DOG'S BEST FRIEND

by
Hank Ketcham

FAWCETT GOLD MEDAL • NEW YORK

DOG'S BEST FRIEND

A Fawcett Gold Medal Book
Published by Ballantine Books
Copyright © 1982 by Hank Ketcham Enterprises, Inc.
Copyright © 1979, 1980 Field Enterprises, Inc.

All rights reserved under International and Pan-American Copyright
Conventions, including the right to reproduce this book or portions thereof.
Published in the United States by Ballantine Books, a division of Random
House, Inc., New York, and simultaneously in Canada by Random House of
Canada, Limited, Toronto, Canada.

ISBN 0-449-14490-9

Manufactured in the United States of America
First Ballantine Books Edition: September 1982

10 9 8 7 6 5 4 3 2 1

"I THINK MAYBE RUFF IS GONNA NEED A **LAWYER**, MOM!"

"WHY ARE CATS AN' DOGS SO **EASY** TO UNNERSTAND... AN' PEOPLE SO HARD?"

"HE'S GOT A LOT OF **EVERYTHING** IN HIM."

"WELL, IF IT'S NOT GONNA MAKE RUFF JUMP UP IN THE AIR, HOW COME THEY CALL IT A **BOOSTER** SHOT?"

"RUFF'S PAPERS? NAW...HE ONLY HAD 'EM WHEN HE WAS A PUPPY. WE THREW 'EM OUT SOON AS HE GOT HOUSE-BROKE."

"WELL, WHAT DO YA WANT ME TO DO? TELL RUFF TO MAKE HIS FRIENDS WAIT OUTSIDE IN THE **RAIN**?"

"WHO CAN SLEEP WITH ALL THAT MUNCHIN' GOING ON?"

"WHEN HE GETS OUT, WE'LL HAFTA FILL IT AGAIN...
HE TAKES ALL THE WATER WITH HIM."

" MAYBE I'LL **NEVER** GO TO SCHOOL ...MY FOLKS KEEP TELLIN' ME NOT TO BE SO SMART."

"HOW 'BOUT TRADIN' THESE FOR SOMETHIN' I CAN **TALK** TO?"

"MATT SAYS THERE'S **NO WAY** YOUR PIES COULD TASTE AS GOOD AS THEY SMELL...AND I SAID YOU COULD PROVE IT."

"...AND DON'T WORRY ABOUT THE FLOOR...
RUFF'S CLEANIN' THAT UP."

"I DIDN'T BRING YOUR OL' BOWLIN' BALL DOWNSTAIRS...
IT BRUNG ME!"

"THERE MUST BE **SOME** WAY WE COULD BLAME IT ON THE OIL COMPANIES."

"IF YOU GUYS WAS A TV MOVIE,
I'D **TURN YA OFF!**"

"NAW...THAT'S NOT A WILD ANIMAL GROWLIN'.
MR. WILSON MUSTA SEEN US COMIN'."

"I THINK I'M GETTING 'LLERGIC TO CARROTS, I HOPE."

"HOW'D YOU LIKE TO BE THE JOLLY GREEN MIDGET?"

"REMEMBER **ME**? YOU USED TO BE MY SITTER!"

"YOU WERE WONDERING WHY I CHOSE A CAREER INSTEAD OF MARRIAGE?"

"THAT'S WHY THEY CALL 'EM **LEAVES**, JOEY....THEY'RE ALL THAT'S LEFT OF SUMMER."

"THAT **MESS** YOU'RE TALKIN' ABOUT IS MY **LIFE**!"

"LET ME KNOW WHEN YOU'RE RELAXED ENOUGH TO
HEAR ABOUT SOMETHIN' THAT HAPPENED TODAY."

"THAT WASN'T A SHOT...IT WAS MR. WILSON'S FRONT DOOR."

"LOOKIN' ON THE BRIGHT SIDE ... IT'S A GOOD THING I HAD MY PANTS ON!"

"OBOY!"

"CHOCOLATE CREAM. FOR A MINUTE THERE, I THOUGHT IT WAS MY FROG."

"WHAT'S A VEG'TARIAN?"

"**YUK**! THAT'S THE WORST THING I *EVER* HEARD!"

"FRANKLY, MRS. MITCHELL, I THOUGHT DENNIS' MOTHER WOULD BE A MUCH MORE *WEARY*-LOOKING WOMAN."

"IT **IS** A MATTER OF LIFE OR DEATH ... I DROPPED THE GOLDFISH BOWL!"

"DID YA KNOW THAT WAS MY DAD WHO FELL ASLEEP AN' YELLED 'FORE'?"

"Awwwwww... I dreamed you was makin' **FUDGE**!"

"Boy! When I get my own house, this is the kinda kitchen I'm gonna have!"

"IT'S SURE RELAXIN' TO BE AROUND PEOPLE WHO DON'T WORRY ABOUT GETTIN' FAT."

"INSTEADA GETTIN' MAD AT OL' RUFF, YOU SHOULD BE HAPPY YOUR **FEET** WASN'T IN 'EM!"

"BOY! I BET THIS IS THE BIGGEST FORGIVING ANYBODY EVER ASKED FOR."

"SORRY, DAD... I TRIED NOT TO LAUGH BUT IT CAME OUT MY **NOSE**!"

"...AND IF WE RUN OUTTA GAS, I CAN RIDE FOR HELP!"

"CAREFUL! I BEEN TRAININ' RUFF TO BE A GUARD DOG!"

"BOY, ONE LOOK FROM **HER** AN' YOU 'FORGET EVERTHING I **TAUGHT** YA!"

"IT'S CALLED A 'SMOKE ALARM'. DAD PUT IT UP THERE SO I CAN'T FIX MY OWN BREAKFAST."

"I THOUGHT YOU SAID YOU DIDN'T HAVE ANY TIME FOR FOOLISHNESS!"

"I DON'T MIND ODD-EVEN DAYS FOR GAS....LONG AS WE DON'T HAVE 'EM FOR *PEANUT BUTTER!*"

"DOESN'T ANYBODY EVER LIVE HAPPILY EVER AFTER *WITHOUT* GETTIN' MARRIED?"

"WHY DON'T YA WRITE TO THE PRES'DENT AN' TELL HIM 'STEAD OF A 'LECTRIC BLANKET, EVER'BODY OUGHTA HAVE A DOG AN' A CAT!"

"THAT REALLY BUGS ME! ALL THEM TOTAL STRANGERS WORRYIN' ABOUT MY **TEETH**!"

"DENNIS MITCHELL? SORRY, I DON'T KNOW HIM."

"YOU WOULDA SAID THE SAME THING IF YA KNEW WHAT SHE WAS CALLIN' ABOUT!"

"OOOH...WHAT A BOOFUL LI'L KITTUMS."

"PERSONALLY, 1 WOULDA *SCRATCHED* YOU."

"LOOK AT THAT...ALL THAT MUD JUST GOIN' TO *WASTE!*"

"I DON'T QUITE KNOW HOW TO TELL YOU THIS."

"THERE MUST BE A BETTER WAY OF SAYIN' IT."

"ISN'T THAT *GREAT*? THE DOCTOR SAYS HE DON'T
HAVTA COME BACK ... *EVER!*"

"WHAT HAPPENED? YOU MISSED DINNER."

"I JUST CAME OVER FOR DESSERT."

"You got a **LOT** to learn about girls."

"I got a lot to learn about **EVER'THING!**"

"NOW *THIS* IS WHAT I CALL A **LIVIN' ROOM**, JOEY!"

"HI. WHOSE KID ARE YOU?"

"HIS."

'WHY CAN'T YOU BE **POLITE**, LIKE YOUR FRIEND, MATTHEW?"

"HE'S GOT **HIS** BAG AND I GOT MINE."

"THREE HOTDOGS, THREE ROOTBEERS AND THREE PIECES OF CAKE...NOW THAT'S **MY** IDEA OF A BALANCED MEAL!"

"IT'S AMAZIN' HOW MUCH TROUBLE A LITTLE THING LIKE A **RAZZBERRY** CAN GET YA INTO!"

"WOULD IT HELP IF I **CALLED** BEFORE I COME OVER, MR. WILSON?"

"IF HEAVEN IS THAT PRETTY ON THE BOTTOM, THINK HOW IT MUST LOOK ON **TOP**!"

"YOU DIDN'T REALLY *NEED* A NEW RIBBON, DAD. THERE'S PLENTY OF INK LEFT IN THIS OLD ONE!"

"I SAT ON MR. WILSON'S LAP...FOR ABOUT THREE SECONDS."

"THAT'S *FUNNY* . . . TODAY WE'RE STUFFIN' **HIM**,
AND TOMORROW HE'LL BE STUFFIN' **US** !"

"Dewey's havin' meat loaf. His Dad says some Arab is eatin' *THEIR* Thanksgivin' turkey."

"MR. WILSON SAYS THIS USED TO BE A NICE, QUIET NEIGHBORHOOD... BUT THAT WAS BEFORE MY TIME."

"MAYBE WE SHOULD HANG UP SOME OF THOSE TAKE-A-NUMBER TAGS LIKE THEY GOT AT THE BAKERY."

"WHEN THERE'S COWBOYS AN' HORSES, IT'S CALLED A *WESTERN*.
WHEN THERE'S JUST PEOPLE AN' LOTSA GIRLS, IT'S CALLED
A *EASTERN*."

"I GOT IN A GOOD FIGHT WITH TOMMY, MR. WILSON CHASED
ME HOME AGAIN AND MARGARET SAID SHE HATES ME...
THANK YOU, LORD, FOR A PERFECT DAY."

"MY MOM GETS BOOKS FROM THE LIBERRY, BUT SHE TAKES 'EM **BACK**."

"WHEN ARE YA GONNA GET THE LITTLE MONKEY TO PASS THE TIN CUP?"

"IF YA DIDN'T WANNA TALK TO ME, MR. WILSON, WHY'D YA ANSWER THE PHONE?"

"I GOT EVER'THING READY FOR BREAKFUSS 'CEPT I CAN'T OPEN THE DARN *TACO* SAUCE!"

"I'D RATHER **DROWN!**"

"WE'RE WISHIN' EVERBODY A MERRY CHRISTMAS... 'CEPT THE PEOPLE WHO DIDN'T SEND US CARDS **LAST** YEAR."

"CAN WE WAIT HERE UNTIL HE PICKS IT UP? CAN WE, MOM? HUH?..."

"THIS CORNER WILL BE A LOT WARMER WHEN IT GETS A SANTA CLAUS AND A **KETTLE** ON IT, JOEY."

"WELL, IF YA DON'T WANNA WAKE JOEY, MR. McDONALD, MAYBE **YOU'D** LIKE TO HEAR THE CRAZY DREAM I JUST HAD!"

"IS THERE ANYTHING YOU DON'T WANT FOR CHRISTMAS?"

"WE BETTER START A NEW LIST."

"HOLD IT, JOEY! GIVE HER A CHANCE!"

"OKAY, MARGARET...WHAT DUMB THING WAS YOU SAYIN' ABOUT SANTA CLAUS?"

"MAYBE YOU COULD HITCH A *TRAILER* ONTO YOUR SLED!"

"THE THING MARGARET DON'T BELIEVE IN MOST OF ALL IS TAKIN' CHANCES."

"HAS DENNIS DECIDED WHAT HE WANTS FOR CHRISTMAS?"

"POINT TO SOMETHING."

"I DON'T MIND WATER WHEN IT
COMES WRAPPED FOR CHRISTMAS."

"MR. WILSON SAID HE HOPES I GET SOME COAL IN MY CHRISTMAS STOCKING....WHAT'S **COAL**?"

"MOM!"

"HE WANTED TO ADD A P.S. TO HIS SANTA CLAUS LETTER."

"WHATTA *NIGHTMARE!* OL' SANTA WAS ASKIN' ME WHAT I WANTED FOR CHRISTMAS.....AND I COULDN'T THINK OF A **THING!**"

"IF THEY GOT TREES IN HEAVEN, I BET THEY LOOK LIKE THAT!"

"No use me worryin'...if anybody can handle a heavy sleigh in a snow storm, it's gotta be **HIM**!"

"I DUNNO... BUT WHEREVER HE IS BY NOW, I'LL BET HE'S **POOPED!**"

"IT SURE SURPRISED THE HECK OUT OF *ME*! I DIDN'T FIGGER I'D BEEN THAT **GOOD**."

"NAW, THAT'S NOT A GOLD RECORD, JOEY...THAT'S **JINGLE BELLS**, AND IF MY MOM HEARS IT ONE MORE TIME, SHE'S GONNA **SCREAM!**"

"HEY! DIDN'T YOU USED TO BE **BALD**?"

"I THINK I KNOW WHERE MY CATERPILLARS WENT, MOM...
MR. WILSON'S GOT BUTTERFLIES IN HIS STOMACH!"

"WHEREVER YOU'RE HIDIN' IN THERE, MR. WILSON, HAPPY NEW YEAR, ANYWAY!"

"You've spoiled my New Year's record before I even **GOT** one!"

"BUT IT'S JANUARY, MOM! HOW LONG AM I S'POSED TO BE EXCITED ABOUT MY CHRISTMAS STUFF?"

"REMEMBER WHEN YOU USED TO PICK ME UP *WITHOUT* GRUNTIN'?"

"I WONDER HOW THE *REAL* INDIANS GOT THEIR ARROWS DOWN OFF THE CEILING...."

"THAT NOISE IS MY DAD NOT BEIN' VERY
MERRY 'BOUT CHRISTMAS ANY MORE."

"HE SEEMS NICE, BUT ACKSHALLY HE'S A CARROT-PUSHER."

"I JUST THOUGHT OF ANOTHER REASON
WHY I SHOULD HAVE A TURTLE!"

"TAKE A BITE! THEY CALL IT A *PRETZEL*...IT'S JUST A CRAZY, MIXED-UP CRACKER."

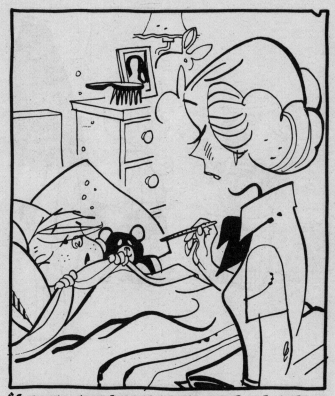

"I DUNNO HOW I CAUGHT THE COLD... I SURE WASN'T CHASIN' IT!"

"COULD YOU 'SPLAIN TO JOEY HOW THIS THING WORKS?"

"EIGHT GIRLS AN' ONLY *TWO* BOYS AT THE PARTY! WE HARDLY GOT A CHANCE TO SAY *ANYTHING!*"

"Mmmmmm! Too bad ya can't slice that smell!"

"BEIN' ABLE TO READ JUST
SPOILS A LOT OF FUN!"

"WHEN YOU SNEEZE, IT MEANS YOU'RE GOING TO KISS A FOOL."

"IT MEANS A BUG FLEW UP MY NOSE."

"*WORSE* THAN CRANKY... SHE'S INTA **MONSTER**."

"WHY DON'T WE LET BYGONES BE BYGONES?"

"BYGONES ARE STILL-HERES."

"THE ONLY WAY TO KEEP HER QUIET IS TO SAY SOMETHIN'
SO **DUMB** IT LEAVES HER SPEECHLESS."

"AW, MOM...IF I START BEIN' POLITE TO MARGARET, SHE'S GONNA START THINKIN' I'M IN LOVE WITH HER OR SOMETHIN'!"

"IT WAS **DENNIS**! WHY CAN'T HE BE AFRAID OF THE DARK LIKE ANY NORMAL KID?"

"DID WE GET HOTDOG AN' RUFF ON A DAY WHEN IT WAS RAININ' CATS AN' DOGS?"

"I KNOW IT HURTS, JOEY, BUT THERE'S NO USE BAWLIN'
'WAY UP HERE WHERE NOBODY CAN HEAR YOU."

"YOU MUSTN'T TALK ABOUT OUR PRIVATE LIFE TO THE NEIGHBORS."

"I DIDN'T KNOW WE **HAD** ONE."

"I LIKED MY **OLD** SUNDAY SCHOOL TEACHER BEST...
SHE WAS CLOSER TO THE BATHROOM."

"YOU BETTER HURRY HOME, MARGARET! IT WOULD BE *TERRIBLE* IF YOU GOT STUCK HERE IN A BLIZZARD!"

"BETTER NOT GET TOO CLOSE TO MOM...
SHE'S GOT CABIN FEVER!"

"I'M NOT HOME."

"I'LL WAIT."

"THERE WE ARE...A NICE HELPING OF MUSHROOMS FOR ME, AND A NICE HELPING OF TOADSTOOLS FOR YOU."

"KNOW WHAT YOU NEED, MR. WILSON? *EXERCISE!*
SO WHY DON'T YA BUILD A INDOOR *SWIMMIN' POOL!*"

"I WAS GONNA SIT ON MR. WILSON'S LAP,
BUT WE COULDN'T FIND IT."

"WOW! LOOK AT THE THERMOMETER! THIS IS A PERFECT MORNING TO HAVE SOME HOT *CHILI* FOR BREAKFAST!"

"IT'S TOO COLD TO STAND AROUND, MARGARET.
WHY DON'T YOU GO HOME AN' I'LL GO HOME!"

"MY DAD ALWAYS FINDS *SOMETHING* TO BE UNHAPPY ABOUT. IN THE SUMMER HE PLAYS GOLF."

"NO, JOEY, WE'RE NOT *MIS'RABLE*... WE'RE HAVIN' A **GOOD TIME**!"

About the Author

Hank Ketcham has been drawing Dennis
the Menace—that all-American favorite
kid—for over thirty years. A musical based
on Dennis's life is scheduled for Broadway
and Hank Ketcham is
co-authoring the script.